Push Your Limits

OrangeBooks Publication

Smriti Nagar, Bhilai, Chhattisgarh - 490020

Website: **www.orangebooks.in**

© Copyright, 2021, Author

All rights reserved. No part of this book may be reproduced, stored in a retrieval system, or transmitted, in any form by any means, electronic, mechanical, magnetic, optical, chemical, manual, photocopying, recording or otherwise, without the prior written consent of its writer.

First Edition, 2021
ISBN: 978-93-90837-41-0
Printed in India

PUSH YOUR LIMITS

PRADNYA JAHAGIRDAR

OrangeBooks Publication
www.orangebooks.in

Preface

I am truly grateful to you for picking up this book. By doing so, you have inched a step closer on a path to achieve your goals and ambitions. You will learn about the simple ways that I respectfully offer you from my learnings and readings over past 30 years.

There are simple life rules which have existed for centuries together from the ancient cultures. These are the rules that I have followed personally for most of my life and I would humbly say, my life has only become better since then. This book is my aim to put them together so that you can benefit from them and learn the value of simplicity, gratefulness, mindfulness and dedication. It is my pursuit to add value to your lives by putting the wisdom together in a simplistic way, which is easy to understand and follow at all the stages of the modern era.

All of us have goals to achieve. These goals could be personal, professional, health-related, financial or spiritual. Some of them are interlinked and depend on the other. For example, after your graduation, you want to secure a job (personal) and then you want a promotion (professional). The very fact that you are reading this book is because you think life is worth it and you want to do more. This book will give you simple yet effective ways on how you can set the right goals and how you can achieve them. This book is for you if you wish to live a happy, meaningful and a content life. And when you look back, you realize you have a life that was worth living.

The words that follow in the forthcoming pages are written from my heart in a deep hope that you will be able to connect with them in every sphere of your life. I would like to learn your reflection of the book and how did you connect with each message. I will look forward to hear from you if you are able to integrate any of these messages in your own experiences. Do write to me on connect@pradnyajahagirdar.com and I will send you a personal note on any topic that you want to discover in detail.

I wish you find hope, prosperity and I pray for you that you may find your life purpose soon. To serve you, is my purpose!

Pradnya Jahagirdar

This book is dedicated to my soulmate, Prasad.

Because of him, I am what I am today. His support, love and encouragement makes me uphold this ancient saying with an important addition in the life of a woman –

"God could not be everywhere so he also created Husbands"

Contents

1. Breathe Better - Live Longer 1
2. Spend 30 Minutes Each Day In Solitude 3
3. Watch Sunrises And Sunsets.................................... 5
4. You Are What You Eat!... 7
5. Which Element Are You? 9
6. Identify Your Flow 11
7. Integrity - Do The Right Thing Even
   When No One Is Watching 13
8. Stand Up For Yourself 15
9. Consistently Keep Plugged
   In To Your Chargers 17
10. The Value of An Elegant Outfit............................. 19
11. Do You Have That Favorite Apparel? 20
12. Dress Up Your Age.. 22
13. Move Around With A Limelight 24
14. Listen To Audio Books.. 26
15. Read - For Your Mind, Heart And Soul................ 28
16. Save At Least 40% of Your Earnings 30

17. Study Before Investing.. 33
18. Learn From Your Kids.. 35
19. Make Time For Your Spouse Every Day................ 37
20. Where Did My Resolutions Go?.............................. 40
21. Always Be Humble And Kind To
    People Lower In Ranks... 42
22. Key To Achieve Big Dreams Is To Dream Big 44
23. Success Is Built Over A Period of Time 47
24. Put Technology To Your Advantage 49
25. Find The Value In Mundane 53
26. Lose To Win 56
27. Remember To Have Fun 59

Breathe Better - Live Longer

Profoundly articulated in the book "IKEGAI" and also from age-old Indian wisdom from the Yoga gurus, the more you focus on breathing better, you will add more healthy years to your lives. In today's world wherein known and unknown stress has become an integral part of our lives, the age-old breathing techniques go a long way in making you calmer, agile and conscious of your own behavior.

Notice that, your breathing is shallow when angry and depressed or in a state of fear or extreme anxiety. Similarly, notice your breathing is deeper when you are listening to beautiful music, when you are bathing, when you are meditating or when you are enjoying with your loved ones. The first step is to notice the difference between the two and consciously reminding yourself to focus on your breath.

Breathe well and you will be less stressed or overwhelmed and eventually learn to let go of what you cannot control. When you consistently and consciously make it a habit to "BREATHE" deeply at least for 30 secs every hour, you will notice the difference in your levels of joy and positivity. And these increased levels add more years to your life. In one of the researches, done at Yale, it was observed that participants who performed controlled breathing exercises experienced the greatest mental health, social connectedness, positive emotions, mindfulness benefits, decreased stress levels and rare depression symptoms.

Spend 30 Minutes Each Day In Solitude

It is important to spend time with people. You learn new things, habits and feel good in the company of interesting people. But too much people time doesn't do any good to you either. Our digital devices make us feel we need to be connected 24/7. All of the noise, chatter and hustle can actually wear you out. They in fact make you feel lonelier than ever.

We keep doing one thing after another and at the end of day realize another day has gone, not giving us any time to do the things we 'wanted' or 'liked' to do. And this gets us into an overwhelming state of mind at the end of the day.

Solitude is crucial to your health and well-being. In fact, the busier you are, more the time you need with your own thoughts.

Being in solitude also doesn't mean you are an outcast or a loner. It just means that you equally value the time spent by yourself and the time you spend with your friends. Spending quality time alone can be restorative. For many people, solitude is like exercising a muscle they had never used. You need to develop it, flex it, train it and learn to use it to your benefit.

Fix a routine, form a habit to be alone for at least 30 minutes every single day. Do this in the 1st hour of waking up or in the last hour before you sleep. You need this time to introspect, plan ahead, learn, review your goals and accomplishments or to journal. The more you introspect, the more you learn and the more you learn, the calmer and wiser you become.

The more you think before an action, the more conscious you are in decision making and behavior. When each action is backed up by a clear line of thought, there is no confusion. Spending 30 minutes in the morning by yourself when the world is asleep, when there are no distractions will give you a great power and will set the magic in your life. When you start making this time for yourself and start reflecting on it each day, you will want to do it more and it would then become your second nature. It will then be difficult not to do this anymore.

Watch Sunrises And Sunsets

If you are a person who easily gets put off by small things, if you have a short temperament, if you are not grateful enough for what you have, start watching the sunrises and the sunsets. They will remind you of the magnificence of the universe - the expanse. You will realize that your worries are so little as compared to it. What do the sunrises and the sunsets remind us of every day? –

SUNRISE

a. The end is the beginning and the beginning is the end;

b. What is up will eventually go down and what goes down will eventually be up, no situation lasts forever;

c. No matter how you feel, get up & show up. The Sun does!! Even if you feel low on a particular day, put in more energy to get up on time, do your chores, do you your workouts, eat healthy and give your best to your family and friends & at your workplace. Being able to follow your routine on harder days will put the mundane work on an auto pilot and you will start doing it without much of an effort. And this will distinguish who you are and what you become over the years.

SUNSET

a. It reminds you of the fragility of life. You are on this planet for a very short time, so do your best before the sun of your life goes down. This feeling alone should put you on a state of urgency, to accomplish as many goals and dreams as quickly as you can;

b. That, if something has not worked today, don't lose hope. Sleep over it and you will find a new way tomorrow;

c. That, eventually, you will get tired. And when you do, you must rest.

You Are What You Eat!

Food gives you pure joy, delight and satisfaction. But what we eat either adds years to our lives, increases productivity while it feels divine or it can make us lousy, lethargic, heavy and sleepy. Any food that is a natural source in itself is divine. Fruits are one of those natural delights - filled with so much goodness of nature, natural sugar, high water content and it just gives you a feeling of WOW when you eat them. They offer you high levels of antioxidants, minerals, potassium and all of those vital sources that you need in a healthy meal.

Start to eat naturally grown and tended fruits, grains and millets and do away with anything that is refined - sugar/flour or anything that comes as a packet and you will notice a remarkable difference in your energy levels. I know it sounds hard but it does get better with time.

Replace 1/2 of your cooked meals with salads, seeds, nuts, fruits and vegetables and watch your energy levels surge like never before. Make your own recipe but remember to stick to the nature. Smoothies or shakes from a combination of nuts and fruits are a few examples. When you start doing this, you will discover a new you that you did not know existed ever. This will also help achieve your ideal body weight. You will lose if you're overweight or gain your optimum if you are underweight. Even further, try not to eat anything after the sunset – yes it works in the modern era too.

One of the secrets why the Japanese are the oldest people living a healthy and disease free life on earth and have a lower mortality rate is, for many centuries they ate only until 2/3rd of the stomach was full. How do you know when you are only 2/3rd full? This is when you can still have a small portion of your meal or that dessert. This is the point when you stop eating. This leaves a good room for digestion. Eat less, eat well and healthy to unleash your core energy.

Which Element Are You?

According to Ayurveda, everything in the universe is made up of five basic elements - Earth, Water, Air, Fire & Ether - the sky. There is further reference available in the Charak Samhita to go deeper into what they are and how their constitution in a combination changes the characteristics of the matter. All of us are the combinations of these elements and the more they are in harmony with each other, the more fulfilling our lives are and this way of living gets us in an equilibrium. The good news about this combination is that there is a theory that defines the type of person you are and ways to alter this with some guidance from an Ayurveda expert.

The journey to finding who we are and what we want to become is very intriguing. For this we need to start observing ourselves as to who we are - am I a short-tempered person, am I always forgiving or intolerant, do I sleep well or most of time I am awake or have a disturbed sleep? Do I feel full of life most of the times?

Do I have a lot of ego? When you start asking yourself these questions and observe your behavior, you start getting your answers on where do you want to go and who do you want to become.

Our emotions are driven by our body compositions and our hormones. If the health condition is not at its optimum, it is because of the imbalance of one or more of those basic five elements. For example, the presence of too much fire element in our body can cause too much anger and acid reflux but if it goes down its optimum level, it causes lack of desire for food, high cholesterol levels, diabetics and lack of creativity. The causes and effects of the imbalance of these basic elements is so subtle that you can't even easily guess or can realize it. When these start to improve, you will only feel better but it is the result of the elements starting to get in harmony and getting more balanced.

Therefore, rather than living the way you are, think of the changed person you want to be. Ayurveda heals both the body and the mind. Besides organic and natural medicines, Yoga and breathing practices are used to increase the balance of these five elements within us.

Identify Your Flow

According to the Japanese culture, everyone has an IKIGAI - a reason for living.

To live a peaceful, joyous and satisfying life, one must get engaged in an activity with a purpose, a reason for getting out of the bed every morning. Something that makes one lose track of time. Flow is a mental state in which one gets so immersed in doing a certain activity, feels fully involved, focused and gets so energized that the outside world completely disappears.

In these times of loud music, chaotic surroundings, sedentary lifestyles and the world moving forward in a rat race, we are killing ourselves day by day by just pushing ourselves to do more and more without pondering if this is what we want and if it makes us happy. When you get into a state of flow, your brain chemical level changes, dopamine is released and it gives you an immense sense of achievement that makes you repeat the behavior.

Identifying what will get you into a state flow is easy - find what interests you or what is your hobby? What is it that helps express you to the core? What makes you feel you have contributed to something for better?Examples - reading a good book, painting, knitting, doing pushups or planks, listening to a finer piece of music, teaching or writing. Once you identify what gets you into a flow, start doing it at least 30 minutes a day and you will find yourself in a happy state of mind, more refreshed and satisfied with your life.

Integrity - Do The Right Thing Even When No One Is Watching

To get into a habit of always doing the right thing, just be conscious of the two key facts - is this the right behavior for me & for people around me and will I regret it later? Being conscious of always doing the right thing will be one of the key stepping stones of you becoming the best version of yourself.

You will experience higher level of inner calm, peace of mind and then the days, the weeks, the months and the years of this behavior will make you reveal and unleash the best version of you. We see a lot of people littering around the public places, spitting on the roads, stealing things from small shops, stealing stationary from workplaces. And they keep doing this thinking no-one is watching. Result? - You know it.

The wellbeing of a home, a town, a city or a country depends on the behavior and integrity of its residents and citizens. Therefore, it is not only the social but also the moral code of conduct for each individual to keep doing the right thing every single day. Remember right is right even when nobody is right.

Stand Up For Yourself

I f you don't, who else will? You are the best judge and confidante of yourself. We are all surrounded by people with diverse cultures and mindsets. Some of them are stronger than others when it comes to common conversations, when making policies, when forming a new process or while designing something new. If you have a disagreement, stand up, speak for yourself and voice out your views. It could happen that others may not have the same views but when you present it based on your experience and give a rationale, it could become a welcome suggestion and accepted as a decision. All of us need to learn the art of expressing ourselves everywhere - in social gatherings, at home with your families and friends, at your workplaces, at local clubs or at any event which involves people at large.

This also stands to protect and safeguard you. Never fall victim of any kind of harassment - physical or emotional. If you don't feel someone's behavior is correct and makes you uncomfortable, speak up. If a coworker taps your shoulder every-time you are in a conversation, tell him or her that it is not an acceptable behavior for you. When you get bullied by someone at your school or college, report it to the authorities. If you hide that uncomfortable feeling or are fearful to report, you will need to bear with it forever. No one else would ever know what you are going through and that an environment is turning up more and more hostile day by day. Speak up now even if your voice shakes. If you don't, no-one ever will and you never will.

Most of the people, most of the times, keep their feelings to themselves in a fear of rejection, of being judged or out of a fear of simply not fitting in. As we age, we must learn to express ourselves in the most polite, humble yet assertive manner. And for people in designated positions, they assume a great responsibility to create an open environment where everyone can freely express themselves. We must start encouraging everyone to speak their minds so it forms a habit over a period of time- from parents to their kids and from leaders to subordinates and peers. Maya Angelou, a renowned poet, an activist and an author said 'Develop enough courage so that you can stand up for yourself and then stand up for somebody else'

Consistently Keep Plugged In To Your Chargers

The battery life of our laptop increases when we keep it plugged while working. Some of the devices won't even work without plugging! When we get up, we plug in all our devices until they are 100% charged. We know once they are fully recharged, they will serve us for the rest of the day. What happens to us? Do we ever care to recharge ourselves every single morning? Again, like every device needs a different kind of a charger so do we as we are all different human beings. Find your own way to fully recharge yourself at least once a day and you will notice an increase in your productivity, inner calm, peace, composed behavior and joy. They could be any one of the below but it really depends on what resonates the best with you –

a. In the first 10 mins of waking up, think about at least 10 things you are grateful for

b. Recite your goals and read out your most powerful affirmations
c. Go for a 30 min walk or a jog
d. 30 min yoga session
e. Chanting sacred sounds or meditating for 30 mins

When we use the first hour of our waking up recharging ourselves, it gives a phenomenal advantage to think better, plan, reflect, introspect, assess and empower ourselves for the day ahead of us.

Do you remember a day when you shut your alarm off and woke up late and then everything just got delayed one after the other? You had no time to plan, you missed your breakfast or your train, got delayed to work or school, missed that meeting, were late for the lecture and the things after. You then felt worn out and tired, why? How did you feel at the end of that day? Lost in directions? Overwhelmed? Caught up between many things? No time for yourself? All of this happened because your battery was overused and eventually ran out of the charge. It indeed was constantly reminding you to recharge yourself before finally shutting down.

10

The Value Of An Elegant Outfit

Do you absolutely love what you wear every day? If you don't, it's time to change your wardrobe. There is so much energy and confidence that flows in your existence and gives your aura a great positivity when you are dressed up well every single day! The outfits you select don't necessarily need to cost you a fortune. They could be simple and yet very elegant but most importantly, they make you feel so good about yourself. It could be the effect of the fabric that adds a lot of comfort or that color or the way it is tailored, its length or just its simplicity.

Try this consciously and you will notice changes in the way you carry yourself in the most affluent ways you would ever do.

Do You Have That Favorite Apparel?

Ever noticed how confident, poised and good you feel when you wear your most favorite apparel? Why? Because that gets you into a winning mindset and makes you feel super confident. You feel sky is the limit.

My favorite apparels vary depending on where I am heading to. For example, I like to wear that jump-suit on a holiday, I end up wearing that shirt for most of my interviews, and I go back to that beautiful dress when I am out with my spouse for a long drive. The reason I do this is because, I associate being myself in a particular way while wearing it. Have at least a couple of those most loved outfits in your closet to give you a feeling of empowered, in control, confident, on the edge and you will know beforehand that you would have had the best of yourself in a meeting, in an interview or on a date.

Remember you must feel happy and relaxed in what you wear and your clothes must appear to be a part of you.

12

Dress Up Your Age

Taking your 'favorite apparel' further, always be conscious to dress up your age. You can play with colors at all ages yet be mindful of the shades, the fitting and the way you carry it. What you wear must complement your age, your body language, your appearance, strength and your maturity. Your outfits also speak about your authority and decision making power.

If you have a good aesthetic sense, choosing what to wear is a simple decision. If you are the one who is thinking of adding more exuberance to your personality by choosing what to wear, think of your hero or your inspiration - who do you want to be? Who do you want to look like? It will benefit if this ideal person is near-about your age. Now look into the mirror and compare if what you wear matches to the personality you have in your mind. And this thinking will guide you on what to wear. You will now start synchronizing the color, the texture, the fabric and how you feel when you wear it.

The way you look, feel and carry yourself adds an aura to your personality. Your look is not your clothes alone but how do you accessorize yourself too. Always do your hair that complements your outfit. Wear your glasses that go well with your outfit and your hair. Select a footwear that complements your outfit. For females, coordinate your accessories - your neck piece, your ear rings, your scarfs, scrunchies and your handbags with your outfits. For men, coordinate your outfit with your jackets, ties, belts, wallets, your socks and your scarfs. These are very small and subtle changes in the way you dress up. Being conscious about what to wear will make a huge difference to your persona.

Let us aim to look our age - not below, not above. And how nicely said by William Somerset "The well-dressed man is he, whose clothes you never notice".

13

Move Around With A Limelight

Even a thought of being in limelight releases the dopamine, isn't it? When we are conscious of who we are, what is our life goal, what do we stand for, what do we take pride in and we are able to exhibit all of this in our behavior, our aura magnifies. It adds grace, poise and cheer to the way we walk or the way we carry ourselves. Did you ever see a confused or a depressed person walking with a head high, his back upright and a reassuring calm on the face? No!

How does it feel being under limelight? It feels you are guided by forces and power from above, you are being guarded and protected and you feel worthy. When you feel low, get up and think about at least 5 things you are grateful today and say 'thank you' as you take your steps. Imagine you are surrounded by a divine limelight around you and see the magic happen. Being consciously under this secret magic limelight brings you back to your own deepest nature - You.

You will be delighted, confident, attractive and most importantly, you will captivate those around you with happiness and joy because of your aura.

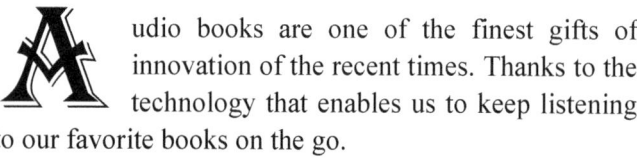

Listen To Audio Books

Audio books are one of the finest gifts of innovation of the recent times. Thanks to the technology that enables us to keep listening to our favorite books on the go.

They work especially well when you club them with a monotonous activity or pair it with an exercise routine - during your walk or in the gym, cooking, cleaning up your house, on your drive to and from work, on a plane or a train or bus, while you wait in a queue for your turn at the bank or at college, just anywhere. What a beautiful idea to make the best use of your time! While most of the commuters or people waiting in the queues are getting frustrated over the traffic, to turnaround time at the counter, you are happily finishing that next amazing book.

There is so much to read and there is unfortunately no time to get a paperback and get lost into it. In the book, "Atomic Habits", James clear points out a nice strategy to cultivate a new habit. He says you can combine a "need" and a "want" to form a new habit. For example, if you want to check Facebook updates (want), you make it a point to do that after you have meditated for 30 seconds (need). You can start listening to audio books when you are doing your mundane chores. And when you form a habit of doing this and learn the trick to do both, you will have "read" your most favorite books by the end of this year. Could be 10 -20-30??

Off course you can still grab that paperback for your collection if you loved that audio book. If you are super busy, by listening to the audio books this year, you will have heard your favorite books already and it is so much more value as compared to waiting to find time "reading" a book.

15

Read - For Your Mind, Heart And Soul

s author Ama Dunedin says "Books are the planes and the train and the road. They are the destination and the journey. They are home". The more we read & write, the more we discover ourselves. Magic happens when we read. Each book comes your way at the perfect time of your life when you need it the most. The wisdom comes in a form of an answer to a question you have been waiting to find for long.

The connection between the mind, heart and soul is so subtle and thin and a good book helps keep it connected. Buying good books and creating a massive library is a huge and a lifetime investment. This is that precious corner of your home which gives so much pride and joy. The books you read are the predictor of the kind of person you are and who are you in the making. Getting immersed into a book is as good as a meditation - to achieve a state of flow. Other reasons emphasizing the importance to read -

a. You have a really short time to live on this planet and you cannot spend time making all the mistakes and learn from them. A biography helps you learn experience of other people on the same path
b. Way to knowledge
c. Way to the mastery of a particular subject
d. Wisdom
e. Education
f. Entertainment

I have some books in my collection that I keep going back to again and again. No matter how many times I read it, I get a different perspective every time as if I am reading it only for the first time. This happens because the book is the same but how you resonate it with it depends on your current state of mind, your heart and soul. The book hasn't changed but you have!

16

Save At Least 40% Of Your Earnings

The richer remain the richest and the poor remain the poorest. The reason this happens is because a rich person's inclination is first to save and later spend the remaining. Whereas a poor person is waiting to receive the money to be spent leaving very little or nothing to save. The outcome is clear, the investor will remain invested and a poor person will have expensed out most of the earnings.

Follow the basic rule 40/40/20 as a guide to spend your money. Here it is -

1st 40% of your income	Investments
Next 40% of your income	"NEEDS" - groceries, phone/internet, basic clothing, fuel, parking, utility and maintenance bills
Remaining 20% of your income	"WANTS" - luxury vacations, expensive clothing and shoes, premium cars, luxury watches and accessories, expensive club memberships

When you observe carefully, you will notice when a poor person gets additional money, he will tend to spend all his money on 3rd category- on what he "wants". And by doing so, he thinks himself to be a rich person. Whereas a wise investor, on a sudden financial gain will tend to invest a substantial portion into the 1st 40% category. We live in an economy where inflation is always on the rise, prices of fuel and other basic necessities are only surging to new highs every day, we must learn to invest wisely to secure our future. After 20 years, the money you will need to meet your NEEDS would have grown substantially and you will need to start investing now to reap the benefits compounding. Assuming the simple rate of interest on government bonds is 6%, if you invest Rs.60,000 a month for 15 years, you would have accumulated a corpus of Rs.1.8 cr. The present value of this Rs. 1.8cr is Rs. 70 lacs at 6% discounted rate. Does this fact scare you enough? The healthcare expenses are ever skyrocketing and if anything goes wrong, it will put an enormous strain on your savings. Warren Buffet says "If you buy things, you do not need, soon you will have to sell things you need". When you make saving a habit from every single financial gain you make, you are securing and safeguarding your future. The more you save in your early years, the more you will relax in your later years.

Remember as you age, the 40/40/20 rule will need to be modified to 50/40/10 and later 55/45/10. And if you can follow these rules of staying invested throughout to at least 50%, your wealth will become at least 2000 times over a period of 20 years. This is the rule that the millionaires and the billionaires follow.

17

Study Before Investing

Taking the cues from previous chapter of investing at least 40% of your earnings, where to invest is the crucial decision. Suggestion - from your first 40% category, save 50% of it into bonds, government and debt funds, securities and fixed income deposits. The next 30% will go into long term large cap equities which are currently trading below their fair value and the remaining 20% goes into those stocks which are extremely aggressive meaning they give you high returns coupled with high risks. Let us assume 40% of your money that you want to invest this year is 1,00,000 and let us calculate how much money you will make at the end of the year. 50% of fixed income savings will yield you a return of 6% equivalent to Rs 3,000 (1,00,000 x 50% = 50,000 x 6% = 3,000). Large cap equities will give you an average return of 15% (depending on market yield) meaning a return of 4,500 (1,00,000*30% = 30,000 x 15% = 4,500) and the next 20% which is the 20,000 could become zero or could also become 20,000,000 at the end of the year. And when you keep investing your 1,00,000 for 20 years/30 years, imagine the value of your investments and this will easily make you a millionaire. If you are interested to know my strategies for investing in detail to learn how and where to invest your last 20% to reap the benefits of high margins, please write to me on

connect@pradnyajahagirdar.com

The key to overall investment strategy is to keep invested for a long period. Stay invested for decades and watch your portfolio grow exponentially after 30 or 50 years. That's the magic of staying invested in the longer run.

18

Learn From Your Kids

Indian spiritual leader and author Sadhguru Jaggi Vasudev says 'When a child enters your life, it's the time to learn (not the time to teach). So true!

What can we learn from a child? Love unconditionally, never hold off to express your awe, your joy and your anger. When you get emotional, cry! Laugh your heart out in funny moments, play, play and play until you are panting and tired. Eat less, never lie and be full of life all the time.

If you want to be truly happy, let loose at times and be a child again. Playing with children teaches you how to easily forgive, they help you win and teach how to support each other and they motivate you. They hold your hands and they hug you when they are overwhelmed. Watching your kids grow and spending time with them adds joy to our life. It enriches our life by leaps and bounds.

Parents like to think the kids need them in their early years but the truth is we need them more than they need us. Treasure your moments with your child as these small wonders will quickly grow up by the blink of an eye. You will still have your work and your office and your chores as you get old. But if you prioritize it over spending time with your child, you will not realize how fast your child would have moved into adulthood. Rather than the child, the one who will miss their childhood the most will be you. Seize those golden moments, make happy memories, be available when they need you - to play, to run and to hug them when they are scared.

Sometimes, the only thing a child wants is being around their parents, nothing more. Think of the ways you can schedule time with your kids - it could be playing in the garden in the morning or Saturday evening stroll in the park or playing hide and seek on a Sunday afternoon. Your kids will remember these moments when they grow up. And if you lose these moments today, you will lose them forever. Everyone gets too busy with their own lives, so will your kids, one day.

Make Time For Your Spouse Every Day

A life and a house run well when a couple has great respect for each other, when they are each other's best critics, best friends and the lifetime companions. A relationship in which each person draws enormous energy & power in each other's company, feels supported, taken care of, respected and looked after, all other areas in life for those two people will automatically get influenced in a positive way. Your happy and content relationship with your spouse is the rock-solid base for everything else in your life. Sheryl Sandberg in her book 'Lean In' shares an important experience of her life – "make your life partner your partner in everything". When you do this over years and decades, you will see your lives together would have become happier & satisfying.

Your parents will always have the generation gap when you are in a conversation with them, your kids will be too young to understand your perspective and they might even look up to you as their role models. Of course, you have your friends but everyone is busy with their own life. Your partner, if you together make each other your confidante, your best buddy, you will always have a friend for your life.

A matured and a supported relationship will give you tons of confidence, the power to overcome any difficult situation - emotional & physical. When you both help each other finding your best in each other, supporting through the ups and downs and just being there for each other, your personal relationship will become your lifeline. Yes, we are all buried in our professional lives but the more time you make for your most intimate relationship, the more peaceful, happy and successful you become.

Spend at least 30 minutes every day together, free from all distractions. It need not be 30 minutes at one stretch but could be little breaks spread out during the day. Examples could be sipping your morning tea together, discuss your day ahead, planning your next vacation, your finances, discussing your child's growth. It could also be a 2-minute phone call after your lunch or 15 minute walk together, post your supper to talk about your day. Remember men and women have different needs. A man craves for physical intimacy and a woman craves for emotional. It is about finding, creating and maintaining the balance.

There is no thumb rule to make your spouse your bestie as each individual is at a different stage of his and her life. Being open, friendly, nonjudgmental, just being there available for each other, offering support without asking are some of the fundamental yet monumental stepping stones of a rock solid yet the most beautiful and magical relationship.

20

Where Did My Resolutions Go?

The reason you are reading this is because you wish to invest in yourself and you wish to discover your true potential. You always knew you had it within you. The time to act is NOW. Carefully articulate at least these 6 resolutions this year to begin your journey to success and wellness -

1. Health - make time to exercise each day, especially on your most busiest days
2. Food - reduce your food to 2/3rd, and make it 50% of fruits, vegetables and nuts and the remaining can be cooked food. Eat only when you are hungry
3. Family - to save at least an hour of each day to spend with your family. It could be a family meal, a prayer together for a stroll or anything that lets you spend your 100% undistracted time with your loved ones

4. Financial - to make sure you invest at least 40% of your annual income this year

5. Self-development - pick up a development area. It could be learning a new language so that you can speak to your customers better for the continent your work for. Or it could be learning to cook, learning how to invest in stock market, and learning to speak in public or anything that you have always wanted to learn. Prioritize what do you want to learn and put in a schedule or pay in advance for the trainings and courses to make sure you don't lose the momentum half way

6. Serve others - it could be to resolve to always be empathetic to people, it could be encouraging someone achieve their goals, it could be funding education for a kid in need, it could be supporting a cause that aims to save nature. Find the one, that resonates with your heart and do it this year. You will then discover the joy of giving.

To make sure these resolutions do not just stay in your mind, print them and stick them at a place you see often during the day. Review their progress in your quiet time - early in the morning or last thing before you sleep at night.

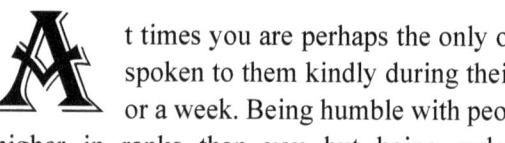

Always Be Humble And Kind To People Lower In Ranks

At times you are perhaps the only one who has spoken to them kindly during their entire day or a week. Being humble with people who are higher in ranks than you but being rude to others, especially the less fortunate tells a lot about you.

It is very easy to be rude to the sanitation workers, your house help, your driver, the janitor. You will find many people in the world who are insensitive to the value they add to our lives by doing the hard work that nobody wants to do. A janitor helps us with clean, nice, dust free surroundings and odor free spaces. A driver takes upon himself the stress of driving into a bad traffic so you can sit back and relax, listen to beautiful music, read, work or to talk to someone you love. Your house help, without them you will spend so much time doing the chores yourself and be so drained leaving you no time to do the things you wish you did.

Do we recognize how grateful we are to have those community helpers around us? Let us consciously try and BE!

22

Key To Achieve Big Dreams Is To Dream Big

You can dream big only when you have the mental freedom to think of what do you want from life. This is possible when you are able to leave aside all the reasons why can't you make it a reality. If your dream is not the one that just even thinking of achieving it blows you off, it is not a dream big enough. Remember it is only the clarity of thoughts and determination to pursue decides how quickly a dream can manifest. You will go only so far in your life as your dreams. If you see yourself as an ordinary person, living an ordinary life, this what you will end up to be. If you see yourself as a highly successful person, living a life filled with love, luxury and abundance, so will you be. Remember you are the creator and mental custodian of your dreams. It is not for others to help you achieve them or give you 1000s of reasons of failure. If you believe in your dream, you will need to constantly guard it until it becomes a reality.

It is also true that any dream will not manifest by itself without an action. Draft a plan and break it into several achievable steps. Constantly check if you are on the path where you wanted to be, if not make corrections. Every single step matters in achieving your journey of thousand miles.

Ways to turn your dreams into reality –

1. Believe in yourself;
2. Take consistent actions;
3. Set a timeline;
4. Ignore the naysayers;
5. Don't worry too much about perfection;
6. Tell others about it but don't wait until everyone agrees with it;
7. Celebrate small wins;
8. Never give up;
9. Get outside of your comfort zone. You will soon realize what your true potential is;
10. Be too strong to let fear creep in;
11. Living small is hardly inspiring ;
12. Don't wait until the situation, economy, weather or anything else to turn perfect. It never will;
13. Work hard and don't stop until you finally make it;
14. Get others to work with you;
15. Don't make excuses;

16. It is okay to fail and start over. Fall 10 times and get up the 11th time;

17. Take responsibility for consequences for your actions;

18. Don't underestimate the competition but don't allow it to stop you;

19. Allow a lot of feedback;

20. Constantly evaluate your progress;

Remember, the best time to start is NOW!

23

Success Is Built Over A Period Of Time

The value of daily consistent routines has been proven for centuries. You don't see a blooming flower the night after you sow the seed. Define a goal, set up a plan and a schedule containing daily steps to achieve it. Small consistent steps lead to sustainable results over a long period of time. Taking small steps to achieve your goals is far better than thinking about your goals and building them just in your mind and doing nothing to execute. When you resolve to make an action plan and follow it every single day, you may not be able to see anything majorly changing right away. Don't get disheartened and hold on to patience, to know that your dream is in the making.

As an example, when you start eating healthy and start exercising for 30 mins each day, you may not lose weight in a month or two or three - but you will notice you have changed significantly by the end of the year. Besides losing weight, you will feel energetic, agile, your skin will look suppler, your mood will improve and you will handle stressful situations in a more composed manner. If you want to learn to invest in stocks, you enroll yourself for trainings, watch videos and attend webinars. Start investing small and you would have accumulated good amount of wealth over the years. When you want to learn to start painting, enroll for a painting class, start with carefully looking at the beauty around you for 30 mins every day. Start painting every single day and when you do this over a month and for years and decades, you will have mastered it.

Malcom Gladwell in his book "Outliers", has explained the rule of 10000 hours which he calls the rule of mastering anything. He says, to achieve mastery, you need at least 10000 hours of work on that topic. It could be music, salesmanship, mastering a new language, learning a new instrument or getting fitter.

24
Put Technology To Your Advantage

Human life has both been enriched and distorted by the increasing use of technology and innovation. Who thought of using cloud to store your data 100 years ago? Who thought of a video call to your loved one before centuries ago when birds were being used as messengers? Who thought of using google and navigators while travelling 50 years ago? Google has become our favorite go to resource for any question. Not parents, not teachers, not friends and not ourselves anymore.

Technology has improved our lives in many ways, but are we conscious of the cost of it? And what are we losing? We have more Facebook connections than real life. We like to "LIKE" someone's achievement for a new venture, a new job, or new book. How many times do we really care to call them to congratulate and tell them how proud they make us? Right from a 5-year-old to 80-year-olds, everyone is so busy and happy online that they are left with little time to be in line with their own selves. The technology for sure is a greatest gift to mankind. However, it is meant to serve you, not to control you. Stop letting it steal your time as when it does, you feel overwhelmed. Let us learn to be conscious and use it to our advantage. Below are proven 5 rules that the successful people use to manage the digital distractions -

a. Shut down all gadgets - TVs, phones, laptops at least an hour before bedtime and use this time to play with your kids, to discuss your day with your partner or to plan your next day.

b. Always use social networking sites for increasing positivity. No negativity on internet please. There is enough already and you don't want to add to it.

c. No smartphones, laptops or digital gadgets in the first hour of waking up. You can of course use your device if you want to meditate with your favorite music. But nothing beyond that which will feed your mind with news or messages in the first hour.

d. Always evaluate where you are spending your time that you have saved because of automatic gadgets and equipment around you. Continuously asses if that is the time worth spent?

e. Don't turn on automatic news feeds if you are a person who wants to check every single update

10 examples of technology I put best to use -

1. Listening to guided meditations;
2. Sharing your new learnings and experiences via social networking to inspire and motivate people;
3. Publish a book;
4. Investing at the right time;
5. Keeping a track of your goals, behaviors, and your investments by use of applications. They provide you a very good tracking against your targets - so powerful for reviews, adjusting or changing your course;
6. Improve your health - decide to walk at least 7000 steps a day and your smartwatch will keep a count for you over the days, weeks, months and years. This idea will serve as visual cue to keep motivating you. When you see something improving over a period of time and realize the value of accumulation, you will tend to stick to it, without much effort;
7. Read, read and read - wherever you are, wherever you go and whenever possible;
8. A strict no-no to go games, checking WhatsApp or Instagram or Telelgram every time your phone beeps. Same with checking your other social feeds every time you get a notification
9. James Clear in his book "Atomic habits" has prescribed a very useful trick on how he keeps himself away from social networking and news during his workweek. He simply asks his assistant to change all his passwords for all his accounts and asks

further to create a different password for every account. This makes it so hard to ask for a password, to use it and to check your account. By nature, we tend to defer what is not easy and convenient. If you want to ask for a new password, use it and check your social feed now, you are more likely to prioritize finishing what is in your hands first and put the task of checking your social feeds to later. And later and later. Hola!! Just imagine how much time you will get during the entire week to produce the best of the results. Your levels of productivity and focus will shift to a whole new level!

10. Unfollow - sure, you were following some topics and some people 10 or 15 years ago. Review if those topics and those people have the relevance in your life today. If not, unfollow. This will give you so much space and time to focus on what is important to you - NOW!

Find The Value In Mundane

Mundane work is the ordinary work that in the first instance doesn't appear to be to interesting or exciting. It is important to get great things done but it is important to get the mundane things done too. We can only be at our best when we feel the most comfortable. Being "comfortable" could mean different things, for different people. Mundane work are those chores that broadly define who we are. We become the things we do consistently and repetitively. These are not the things that will get great things done but they are the foundation for getting great things done. Once your daily chores are done, you feel all set for great things in your life.

It is great if you feel encouraged to change the world, build your start up, be innovative, want to bring in technology to improve people's lives but it is so important to be a good mother, a good spouse, a loyal employee, a true friend. It is only when you start valuing the mundane, you will have the emotional readiness to do big things.

For a successful organization, it is important to find new customers but is important to equally serve the existing customers well. It is only when you keep your focus on providing consistent value to your existing customers, you will start attracting prospective customers.

If an organization is preparing for new project, it doesn't mean they can undervalue the importance of the current operations – they must have a solid system in place to ensure the routine, tactical things get done – vendors get paid on time, bank accounts are managed well, collections from customers is not overdue and employees get paid on time.

For successful managers, managing the team and existing stakeholders is equally important as managing prospective stakeholders. When you look after your teams, when you help them achieve their career goals, when you are available for them in crisis situations, they will do everything to deliver on their objectives and they will stand by you. And this will go a long way in serving your customers and stakeholders consistently. This is why it is truly important to stay equally focused on the day-to-day tasks/responsibilities and anything that it takes to keep the show running.

I feel good to drive when my car is ultra clean. I like to get up at 5 am every day and exercise and I don't stop doing it on my most busy days. When I am away for work to a different city or a country, I leave the hotel for work only after I have called my husband and daughter.

If you want to work to achieve your big goals, don't underestimate the value of mundane. Exercise well, eat well, spend time with your family, go to a temple or church, engage into ordinary discussions with people around you and keep doing your ordinary-usual-daily things. They give you a bit of yourselves to enjoy the present moment.

26

Lose To Win

Winning is sure great but if you want to do something big in life, you must learn to accept the failures along the way too. You cannot win all the time and you cannot lose all the time. Because, losing doesn't mean you lost it. It is only after a defeat when you get up, call on your strengths and start over again, you will win your game.

Our defeats are our great teachers. We learn from our failures, mistakes, adversity and setbacks. It is only when we make a note of our learning from those failures with a positive mindset and move forward, we truly win. It is through our experiences that we grow.

Winning is great but losing reminds us that something, someone is potentially bigger, greater and stronger than us. If we were to win all the time, we would become complacent, restful, finding glory in our current success and refusing to grow.

When you lose, don't let it shatter you. If you never tried and never failed, you would not know what doesn't work.

It is only when you try 100 things and only one of them worked, you have learned 99 ways, on how it will not work. Every break through, idea and success in personal development comes from building upon loses and mistakes. Our greatest accomplishments in lives come when we work with dedication, positively and relentlessly towards our goal. This is how we achieve what we thought was impossible for us. Yes, it is unlikely that we achieve success overnight. It is from those consistent steps with great focus, learning from mistakes and knowing where to focus more, will make that dream come true.

When you lose, keep in mind –

1. Success comes to those who keep trying, not to those who refuse to get up when they lose;

2. Competition is good for you;

3. When you lose you become empathetic as you realize how it feels to lose;

4. Loser is the one who stops at one failure. A consistent performer only learns from a failure, becomes even more focused and moves forward;

5. To experience how it feels to Win, you must first experience how it feels to Lose;

6. Remember never to give up;

7. If you learned a lesson, you didn't really lose;

8. Look at the bigger picture and you will realize one small failure has no power to pull you down;

9. Study about your failures, if possible, discuss them with the people you trust. That might open up

multiple dimensions to consider which you never noticed, existed;

10. Keep reminding yourself of your dreams;
11. If someone else is better, it does not mean you are any smaller;
12. Your dream and your hope is worth it;
13. You have a big heart and you can forgive yourself.

27

Remember To Have Fun

What fun does to us? It helps us feel light, emotionally balanced and it reduces stress. Being funny ourselves or with funny people makes us feel full of life, happy and everything suddenly seems light. Your face looks much better with a smile than a frown. Studies show us that healthier people mostly are the fun-loving people. They are energetic, enthusiastic, don't take life seriously and most importantly, they can laugh at themselves! Fun at work increases productivity. Fun in life increases wellbeing and brings contentment.

Think of someone who is always serious. What do you think of him? Boring, always has a straight face, doesn't have even a handful of friends, always chasing something and getting upset if something goes off the track. Now think of a person who has a great sense of humor. How does it feel like with him around? Enjoying life, never be too serious, take it easy and world is not going to end today. When you are with fun loving people, you tend to get distracted from your worries.

Enjoy and live life in the present moment, life moves on too quickly. Laugh before life laughs at you. Create the best memories with the people whom you love the most.

Ways to have fun –

1. Play an indoor or an outdoor game or an instrument, whatever that makes you happy;

2. Let lose;

3. Don't be judgmental;

4. Give yourself and others a benefit of doubt;

5. Start doing things you are scared of;

6. Try new things – cuisines, places, meet new people;

7. You don't need to spend more money, to have fun;

8. You don't need to think what others will think if you have fun. There is no reason to feel guilty or less appropriate if you have fun;

9. You cannot plan to be funny at a certain time or on a certain day. Being humorous is an art that can be cultivated with effort.

www.ingramcontent.com/pod-product-compliance
Ingram Content Group UK Ltd.
Pitfield, Milton Keynes, MK11 3LW, UK
UKHW022211230426
12048UKWH00016BA/775